PELE
Goddess of Hawaiʻiʻs Volcanoes

Collection of Barry E. Moore

Cover painting
Collection of Robert Romer

CONTENTS:

MAHALO!

Helpful friends made this little book more fun to do. Mahalo to Frank Miller for editing assistance; Jack Lockwood of the Hawaii Volcano Observatory for his geological advice; Jon Erickson of the National Park Service as well as Glenn Mitchell and Kathleen English of the Hawaii Natural History Association for looking over the manuscript; and Professors Rubellite Kawena Johnson and Fred Kalani Meinecke of the University of Hawaii for their insights as Hawaiian scholars. Any errors in this work are mine alone.

Alexandra Halsey typeset the text using Apple desktop equipment, and John Rutherford phototypeset the captions. Throughout my infatuation with "the other woman" who is the subject of this book, my wife Deon graciously refrained from any jealous behavior.

Typeset by Halsey Associates, Santa Barbara, CA and Kona Coast Typesetting, Kailua-Kona, HI

Printed in Japan

PELE
Goddess of Hawaiʻi's Volcanoes

Writing, Art, & Design by
Herb Kawainui Kane

The Kawainui Press
Captain Cook, Hawaii 96704-0163

$\mathcal{S}$HE is Pele-honua-mea, Pele of the sacred land. She is Pele-'ai-honua, Pele the eater of land, when she devours the land with her flames.

She rules the volcanoes of Hawai'i, and Mankind has no power to resist her. When Pele is heard from, her word is the final word.

In folklore she may appear as a tall, beautiful young woman, or as an old woman, wrinkled and bent with age, sometimes accompanied by a white dog. When enraged she may appear as a woman all aflame or as pure flame. Her sacred name as a spirit is Ka-'ula-o-ke-ahi, the redness of the fire.

To know Pele is to know the awe that the first Hawaiians must have felt when they came upon this huge island crowned with fiery volcanoes and trembling with earthquakes, an island so different from the smaller and more tranquil islands and atolls they had known in the South Pacific. In this new land they found a force which could send rivers of molten lava to destroy all that men had wrought. Yet it was also a creative force, building new landscapes of stark, massive beauty. In a world where all natural forces were regarded as life forces and personified as gods, Pele was born.

Many of the mysteries of Pele's domain have been explained by scientific inquiry. Today, when mythologies of the past appear to have been largely replaced by a mythology of the future, some may believe that Pele is now dead; for it was once said that the gods of Hawai'i would die when there were no longer any priests to keep them alive, to feed them. So it may be with many of the gods of old Hawai'i; but I have yet to hear a Hawaiian — or a geologist — suggest that it is time to cast Pele into the dustbin of superstitious nonsense.

So long as the earth is alive with quakes and eruptions, Pele will live in Hawaiian hearts and minds as the personification of the natural phenomena of volcanic activity. She is perceived not through scientific experience but through the emotional experience created by the majesty and power of Hawai'i's volcanoes, and it is this experience that science alone cannot describe.

Tradition states that Pele came, as did the Polynesian discoverers, by sailing-canoe from the ancient homeland in the islands of the Tahiti group. It might be said that she came with them in the form of their capacity to relate to a new and terrifying phenomenon by personifying it. Among some Hawaiian clans in the districts of volcanic activity this relationship is regarded as genealogical, the relationship of an 'aumakua (ancestral spirit) who may take an active role in the affairs of the living. And Pele is indeed active.

Her personality is volcanic — unpredictable, impulsive, given to sudden rages and violence. Hers is both the power to destroy and the power to create new land. Born in the awe experienced by an ancient people, her majestic presence is felt by those who visit her domain today.

"*Tūtū*" is an affectionate term for grandparent, and Hawaiians regard "Tūtū Pele" not with fear but with filial respect; and with a touching resignation should a lava flow consume their homes. In December, 1986, lava destroyed part of the village of Kalapana. A Hawaiian resident, interviewed while loading his possessions into a truck, said:

"I love my home; live here all my life, and my family for generations. But if Tūtū like take it, it's her land."

When picking the *'ōhelo* berries which grow upon high lava fields and cinder plains, older Hawaiians still offer the first fruits picked to Pele before eating any. In the old culture those priests and priestesses who served Pele brought gifts of baked pork, vegetables, fruit, and flowers. But no virgin maidens nor any other human sacrifices were tossed into the crater, despite the stories some romantics love to tell. Accretions of fantasy and mysticism have grown around the image of Pele for which there is absolutely no evidence in Hawaiian traditions.

Nor is it certain that Pele has developed a fondness for distilled spirits, although some visitors to Kīlauea will cast a bottle of gin into Halema'uma'u, the crater within the Kīlauea caldera that is said to be Pele's principal residence. This tradition may have been invented by a former owner of the Volcano House (a small hotel overlooking the Kīlauea caldera) for whom eruptions meant good business. He would ceremoniously present Pele with bottles of gin on Christmas, New Year's Eve, and Mother's Day.

Overleaf: The Discovery of Hawaii
Collection of the Hawaii State
Foundation on Culture & the Arts

POLYNESIAN GENESIS

In the beginning there was only the Darkness, an infinite, formless, black nothingness. But within that void there emerged a Thought, an intelligence that brooded throughout aeons of Darkness over an immensity of time and space.

And in that darkness was created the womb of the Earth Mother whom the ancients knew as Papa. Light was created, the light of the Sky Father Wākea. In their embrace male light penetrated female darkness, and from this union of opposites was created a universe of opposites.

So it was that the Universe was given form and life. For only in the marriage of light and darkness can there be form. And only in sunlight can there be life and growth of living things, all of which must be fathered by light and mothered in the darkness of the womb, the egg, or the soil.

The great gods were born. Kāne the Creator was the first born, and as the eldest he reigned over the others. There was Kanaloa of the Ocean; Kū, who in many guises was patron to the works of men; and Lono, patron of agriculture and healing. These were the male ancestors of all life, the sources of all power. When these gods came to Hawai'i there was a great turbulence of thunderstorms and whirlwinds and blazes of lightning. Their eyes flashed upon the land and the earth shook as they landed upon it.

Also born was the supreme female spirit, the goddess known as Hina in some roles and as Haumea in others, patroness of fertility and of women's works; mother of lesser gods and, as La'ila'i, mother of humankind. Thus the great gods were the ancestors of the people and all other life, and in this way the people were related to all living things. The highest-ranking families were those who were most directly descended from the gods, those chiefly families who kept their blood lines so pure that the *mana* of their godly ancestors, the power that motivates everything in the universe, might flow uninterrupted to them and through them to benefit all their subjects.

Pele was born of Haumea in the ancient homeland. She did not come to Hawai'i until long after the great gods had arrived. Some say that she longed to travel. Others say that she was driven out by a flood. It is also whispered that she was expelled by her elder sister, Nā-maka-o-Kaha'i, who was outraged because Pele had seduced her husband. A goddess of the sea and of water, Nā-maka-o-Kaha'i pursued Pele to Hawai'i.

> *No Kahiki mai ka wahine 'o Pele,*
> *Mai ka 'āina mai 'o Polapola,*
> *Mai ka pūnohu a Kāne mai ke ao lapa i ka lani,*
> *Mai ka 'ōpua lapa i Kahiki.*

> *Lapakū i Hawai'i ka wahine 'o Pele,*
> *Kālai i ka wa'a o Honua-i-ākea,*
> *Kō wa'a, e Ka-moho-ali'i, hoa mai ka moku,*
> *Ua pa'a, ua 'oki, ka wa'a o ke akua,*
> *Ka wa'a o kālai Honua-mea o holo.*

From Tahiti comes the woman Pele,
From the land of Bora-Bora,
From the rising mist of Kāne, dawn swelling in the sky,
From the clouds blazing over Tahiti.

Restless yearning for Hawai'i seized the woman Pele:
Built was the canoe, Honua-i-ākea
Your canoe, O Ka-moho-ali'i, companion for voyaging,
Lashed securely and equipped was the canoe of the gods,
The canoe for She-Who Shapes-the-Sacred-Land to sail in.

PELE'S SEARCH FOR A HOME

In the form of a great shark her elder brother Kā-moho-ali'i, the custodian of the Water of Life, guided the canoe northward. Some of her brothers and sisters sailed with her. Their first landfall was in the northern islands of the Hawaiian archipelago.

Pele needed a deep pit for her home wherein the sacred fires could be protected. She moved down the island chain through Ni'ihau and Kaua'i, digging. But she had been followed from Tahiti by her angry sister, Na-maka-o-Kaha'i of the Sea, and wherever Pele excavated a crater with her digging stick her sister deluged it with water.

Pele then moved farther along the island chain, but each effort to dig a home was flooded out. Thus we find that on the geologically-older island of Kaua'i the craters have become wet swamps, and volcanic evidence becomes progressively more recent as we move down the island chain toward Hawai'i. The myth coincides with the modern geological theory of shifting plates, in which these islands were built in an assembly line as the ocean floor slid northwestward over a "hot spot" in the underlying layer of the earth's crust.

Nā-maka-o-Kaha'i, being Pele's elder sister, was more powerful, for water was believed to be more powerful than fire. Theirs was the eternal opposition between those two elements. Some say that Nā-maka-o-Kaha'i's relentless pursuit ended in a battle near Hāna, Maui, in which Pele was torn apart. A hill named Ka-iwi-o-Pele (the bones of Pele) stands at the site of the battle and is believed to be her mortal remains.

With the death of her mortal self her spirit was freed and elevated to godly status. This event, having taken place in the Hawaiian Islands, made her a goddess native to these islands. Her spirit took flight to the island of Hawai'i where she found a permanent home on Mauna Loa, Earth's largest mountain.

PELE'S FAMILY

Here, high above the sea, the sacred fires could be lighted and kept burning in deep craters without fear of their being quenched by the waters of Nā-maka-o-Kahaʻi. Being female, however, Pele could not make fire. The making of fire was regarded as a male act which women were forbidden to perform. In the Polynesian fire-plow method a length of smooth hard wood is rubbed rapidly within a groove in a softer piece of wood until the friction ignites the wood dust that accumulates at the end of the groove. The keeper of the sacred fire sticks was the god Lono-makua, and with them the fires were made.

*Boys making fire by the
Polynesian fire plow method*

There were also her brothers Kane-hekili, spirit of the thunder; Ka-poho-i-kahi-ola, spirit of explosions; Ke-ua-a-ke-pō, spirit of the rain of fire; and Ke-ō-ahi-kama-kaua, who may be seen in the "fire spears," fountains of lava that thrust warlike from fissures during an eruption.

Pele most respected her eldest brother Kā-moho-aliʻi, who could appear as a man with hands tatooed black or as a great shark, and a king of sharks. He resided in a deep pit at the eastern rim of the world where the sun rises. In his custody was the gourd which held the water of life, water by which the dead could be revived. A promontory at the edge of Kīlauea

Crater is sacred to him, and as evidence of Pele's respect for him the volcanic steam never touches that place.

Among Pele's sisters were Laka, a goddess of fertility and, like Pele, a patroness of the dance. A gentle spirit was Laka, but in another guise she could also appear as Kapo, a goddess of sorcery and dark powers who could assume many shapes at will. A mortal sister, Ka'ōhelo, was transformed upon her death into the *'ōhelo* shrub which flourishes in the volcano region, producing an edible red berry.

But Pele's favorite was her little sister Hi'iaka, spirit of the dance. It is said that she was born in the homeland in the form of an egg, and carried by Pele on the long ocean voyage to Hawai'i under her armpit to keep the egg incubated. Hatched in Hawai'i, Hi'iaka is cherished by Hawaiians as a goddess who is truly Hawaiian despite her origin in Tahiti. As Pele became Hawaiian by the death of her mortal self, Hi'iaka's extended gestation made her Hawaiian by birth.

Pele, Hi'iaka, and Laka were the supreme patronesses of the dance. In the current cultural revival, many dances and dance chants are dedicated to them.

A PANTHEON OF VOLCANO SPIRITS

1. A spirit of rain, moisture, and growing things, **KAMAPUA'A** was in all ways Pele's opposite. Both as enemies and as lovers, theirs was a stormy relationship (see page 27). **KAMAPUA'A** could appear as a man, a gigantic eight-eyed hog, a plant, or a fish.

2. **POLIAHU,** whose white mantle of snow graces the summits of Mauna Kea and Mauna Loa, was a rival to Pele (see page 26).

3. **LAKA** and **KAPO** appear to be two personalities of the same spirit, a sister of Pele (see page 15).

4. **HI'IAKA,** spirit of the dance, was Pele's favorite sister (see page 23).

5. **PELE**

6. **KA-MOHO-ALI'I,** Pele's respected elder brother, a shark god and the keeper of the water of life, led Pele to Hawai'i.

7. **LONO-MAKUA,** keeper of the sacred fire sticks, made volcanic fires at Pele's command.

8. **KA-POHO-I-KAHI-OLA,** spirit of explosions.

9. **KE-UA-A-KE-PO,** spirit of the rain of fire.

10. **KANE-HEKILI,** spirit of thunder.

11. **KE-O-AHI-KAMA-KAUA,** spirit of lava fountains.

JAPAN
NORTH AMERICA
HAWAII
KAUAI
OAHU
MAUI
HAWAII
MARIANAS
PHILIPPINE IS.
MICRONESIA
MARSHALL IS.
CAROLINE IS.
KIRIBATI
POLYNESIA
NEW GUINEA
TUVALU
MARQUESAS IS.
SAMOA
MELANESIA
FIJI
COOK IS.
BORA-BORA
RAIATEA
TAHITI
TUAMOTU IS.
SOCIETY IS.
RAROTONGA
TONGA
NEW CALEDONIA
AUSTRAL IS.
AUSTRALIA
EASTER
NEW ZEALAND

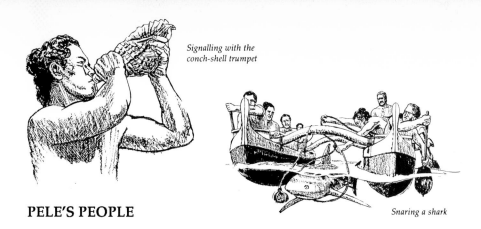
Signalling with the conch-shell trumpet

Snaring a shark

PELE'S PEOPLE

They were a sea people. Having no metals, they developed seaworthy sailing canoes built with stone tools and assembled with lashings of braided rope. These they navigated without charts or instruments over an ocean which was their own and only world, an ocean so vast that it covers half the globe. Here they explored and settled an area equal to the area of the combined continents of North and South America, a vast triangle reaching from New Zealand to Hawai'i to Easter Island. And they accomplished this before European ocean exploration began.

Their food plants, domesticated animals, and language have been traced to an ultimate origin in Southeast Asia, where a Proto-Polynesian people may have been displaced by other peoples — possibly invaders from China — and forced to take to the sea. Finds of ancient artifacts, including pottery fragments of distinctive design, mark a route along the northern edge of Melanesia, an area of islands inhabited much earlier by black peoples.

It is believed that some groups of Proto-Polynesians moved northward from this route into what is now Central and Eastern Micronesia. Those who continued eastward into the Pacific discovered the uninhabited islands of Sāmoa, Tonga, and the eastern islands in the Fiji Group at some time before 1,100 B.C. Here, from perhaps only a few clans, they flourished for over a thousand years in isolation, evolving the physical and cultural traits of the Polynesian people.

About two thousand years ago the exploration of Polynesia was resumed, probably from Sāmoa, by sailing canoes venturing eastward with the winter west winds. The Tahiti Group and the Marquesas Islands were settled, and from there voyages were made which found Hawai'i, Easter Island, and

Behold, Hawai'i!
An island, a people!
The people of Hawai'i
Are the children of Tahiti.

Thus begins Hawai'i's most ancient chant, composed by the navigator
Kama-hu'a-lele as he celebrated his successful landfall at Hawai'i
after a 3,000 mile voyage from Tahiti. The chant praises his chief,
Mo'ikeha, who had sailed from Hawai'i to Tahiti, then returned (above).
The Mo'ikeha Saga includes three generations of Hawai'i-Tahiti round
trip voyaging. A son, Kila, sailed south and avenged an insult to his
father. A grandson, Kaha'i (right), successfully brought young breadfruit
trees to Hawai'i, arriving at Kualoa, Kaneohe Bay, Oahu.

Farming

Plaiting a mat

Dogs, pigs, and chickens were
the only domesticated animals

New Zealand. Hawai'i appears to have been settled at some time before 450 A.D. by voyagers from the Marquesas or Tahiti.

Several centuries later the island of Ra'iātea, near Tahiti, became a center of cultural change and political power. From Ra'iātea and nearby Bora Bora and Huahine, high-status adventurers sailed out in all directions. Hawai'i was rediscovered and conquered, and an era of two-way voyaging between the Tahiti Group and Hawai'i was opened.

Hawaiian traditions appear to begin with this second wave of immigration. The name "Hawai'i" may be traced to Havai'i, the ancient name for Ra'iātea; which may have been named after the largest island in Sāmoa, now called Sāvai'i.

What manner of folk were they? Their myths, legends and social structure were much like those of the Homeric Greeks and Norse Vikings, which are more familiar to most readers. Identification with the clan overpowered any feelings of individuality. Family status was fixed by lineage. Authority was based on seniority, with unquestioning

Decorating tapa (barkcloth)

Chopping with the stone-headed adze

deference given to elders as well as to those senior families whose right to rule was based on being most-directly descended from the greatest gods. The supreme sport was battle. Vengeance was obligatory for any injury done to a kinsman. The exchange of goods and services was regulated by customs of reciprocal gift-giving instead of by trade for profit. A rich store of legend, poetry, and practical knowledge was preserved by trained memories instead of by writing. These are all threads found in the fabrics of ancient cultures. Ancient Greek chiefs (*heroes*) and their Polynesian counterparts (*ariki*) were of the same brotherhood.

Their deities are more accurately defined as ancestral spirits than as "gods" in the modern sense of that term. The greatest of these spirits were the most distant and senior ancestors, the ultimate sources of the powers (*mana*) that gave life to all creatures, motivated all natural forces, and imparted virtues, strengths, and talents to the people. A rigid system of taboos (the term is from the Polynesian *tapu*) was designed to protect this vital flow of *mana*, and thus served as a foundation for laws and social order.

There seems to have been no concept of the supernatural as that term is used in modern religions. Theirs was a universe in which everything (including the gods) was natural and therefore of Nature, an organic universe in which every thing and every person had its integral place within the whole. Success was achieved by living in careful and reverent harmony with Nature, failure to do so being marked by swift retribution from the gods. The modern concept of Nature as an object of conquest would have been incomprehensible to the Polynesian mind.

In all Polynesia, religion so permeated every aspect of life that there was no separate word for it.

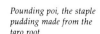
Pounding poi, the staple pudding made from the taro root

THE ROMANCE OF HI'IAKA AND LOHIAU

In a dream, Pele's spirit arose from her sleeping body and travelled from Hawai'i along the chain of islands. Lured by the music of a nose flute she continued on to Kaua'i, where a hula performance was being held at a great platform on Kaua'i's northern shore. There her spirit fell in love with the handsome young chief Lohi'au. Taking the form of a beautiful and sensuous young woman she joined the festivities and won him as her lover.

She stayed with him for several days, while back on Hawai'i her little sister Hi'iaka watched over Pele's sleeping form with growing consternation. When at last Pele's spirit returned to her body she awoke, yearning for Lohi'au, knowing that she must send a messenger to Kaua'i to bring him to her.

Of all her family and retainers only Hi'iaka volunteered to make the journey, for this was in those ancient times when evil spirits and monsters made travel hazardous. Pele was not eager to send her favorite sister on such a dangerous quest, nor was Hi'iaka eager to leave the sacred groves of flowering 'ōhi'a-lehua trees and ferns where she danced with her friend Hopoe, a beautiful spirit of the forest. But Pele was filled with ardent desire for Lohi'au.

Fearing that Lohi'au might be attracted to her sister, Pele exacted a promise from Hi'iaka to refrain from giving him any encouragement. In return, Hi'iaka made Pele promise not to harm her beloved groves or her friend Hopoe while she was away.

Hers was a perilous journey, but Pele had given her powers of sorcery which enabled her to defeat those monsters and spirits that blocked her progress, as well as to assist persons who she found in distress. By trickery, magic, fighting, and with help from friendly spirits, Hi'iaka won her

way from island to island until she reached Kaua'i.

Here she found that Lohi'au had died from grief over Pele's disappearance, but she was able to find his spirit and restore it to his body. They began the return journey.

But the forty days that Pele had allotted for the entire journey had now passed, and Pele, fearing that her sister may have betrayed her with Lohi'au, grew increasingly anxious and jealous with each passing day. At last she became convinced that Hi'iaka had been unfaithful to her trust, and in a great rage she destroyed Hi'iaka's *'ōhi'a-lehua* groves and her friend Hopoe in a torrent of lava.

Although Hi'iaka and Lohi'au were strongly attracted to each other, Hi'iaka had remained loyal to Pele and steadfastly refused his embraces. Not until they approached Hawai'i, and she saw her groves blackened and destroyed and the body of her friend covered by lava, did she know that Pele had betrayed her. Overcome with grief, she took immediate revenge by embracing Lohi'au in full view of her sister. Stung to a fury, Pele attacked with fire and lava. Hi'iaka, having the power of a goddess, could not be hurt, but the mortal Lohi'au was killed.

It happened that a brother of Pele, Kāne-milo-ha'i, was sailing from Tahiti. Approaching Hawai'i he saw Lohi'au's spirit fluttering over the water on the flight which the spirits of the dead all make back to the ancestral homeland. Turning his canoe, Kāne-milo-ha'i reached out, caught the spirit and brought it back to Hawai'i. Here he found Lohi'au's body and restored it to life. On the island of O'ahu, Hi'iaka and Lohi'au were reunited, and together they returned to Kaua'i.

PELE'S RIVAL

The eternal opposition of fire and ice is personified in the rivalry between Pele and Poliahu, goddess of the snow-capped mountain. Poliahu dwells on Mauna Kea, where her white mantle of snow is frequently spread over its crest, and she often invades Pele's territory by covering the top of Mauna Loa with snow.

Geologists list Mauna Kea as an extinct volcano. According to Hawaiian tradition, the extinction was the result of a furious battle between Pele and Poliahu, probably caused by Pele's envy of Poliahu's incomparable beauty and her success in entrancing and seducing handsome young chiefs.

Pele opened the hostilities. She brought all her force to bear on Mauna Kea, causing the mountain to erupt in fountains of fire which melted the snows and drove Poliahu from her home in a panic. But Poliahu recovered her wits and counterattacked, covering the mountain with deep snows, and quenching the fire of Pele at Mauna Kea for all time.

One of the reasons they did not get along was 'Ai-wohi-ku-pua, a romantic but fickle young chief of Kaua'i. In a dream, his spirit courted Laie, a young chiefess of Hawai'i known for her beauty, and made a vow of betrothal to her. He then travelled from Kaua'i to Hawai'i to seek her as his bride. But it was a mission he was never to complete.

As he sailed along the Hāna cost of Maui, he was attracted by a beautiful young woman riding the surf, and turned his canoe to shore. Her name was Hina-i-ka-malama. She fell in love with the handsome stranger, and won his favors in a game of *konane* (Hawaiian checkers). After a brief affair, however, the chief made some excuse and continued on his way.

He did not know that Hina-i-ka-malama was really Pele in one of her human forms. When Pele went into a trance, her spirit could leave her sleeping body and appear in many different guises, each having a different name.

On Hawai'i, while searching for Laie, 'Ai-wohi-kupua was distracted from his quest by Poliahu, who appeared to be even more lovely than the girl he had met on Maui. He courted her, she seduced him, and they became betrothed. He then invoked his personal god to release him from his vow to his first love, Laie, and returned to Kaua'i with Poliahu.

When she heard what had happened, Hina-i-ka-malama pursued the lovers to Kaua'i, where she crashed the wedding celebration, claimed her fickle lover, and won him back.

Now it was Poliahu who was outraged. She punished the lovers with alternating blasts of unendurable heat and cold until they were forced to separate. Hina, we may assume, returned to Kilauea and became Pele again. Poliahu returned to Hawai'i, to her home on Mauna Kea, leaving her inconstant lover with no lover at all, but fortunate to have escaped from the dangerous triangle with his life.

PELE AND KAMAPUA'A

In the Polynesian universe all form was created and distinguished by the pairing of opposites, and perhaps no story better describes this concept than that of the love-hate relationship between Pele and the hog-man demigod Kamapua'a. He could turn himself into a tall, handsome chief with sparkling eyes, often wearing a cape to conceal the pig bristles which grew down his back; or into a gigantic eight-eyed hog. As the occasion required he could also take the shapes of various kinds of fish and plants. With his warclub Kahiki-kolo he could ward off spears and strike down all champions who came against him.

His character personifies the nature of a pig, the largest land animal known to the Polynesians. That which is brought to mind by the modern feminist term "male chauvinist pig" does not fall short of describing Kamapua'a's social behavior and appetites, which frequently got him into trouble. His many amorous adventures and contests with outraged husbands were in the old days told with great relish, and it was said that the entire story of Kamapua'a, recited by a storyteller in courtly style, took as long as sixteen hours to deliver.

Like pigs, Kamapua'a preferred cool damp environments such as are found on the rainy windward sides of the islands, where the stream-eroded gulches and valleys laced with waterfalls are said to have been made by the rooting of Kamapua'a as a great boar. Here too is the abundant vegetation that pigs love, evidence of Kamapua'a's distant relationship to Lono, god of agriculture. In his environmental preferences too, he was the opposite of Pele.

Once when Pele and her sister Kapo were travelling, they were seen by Kamapua'a. Aroused by the sight of Pele, he pursued her. Kapo, however, happened to possess a detachable vagina. To save Pele, she threw this decoy away from the direction of their flight, and Kamapua'a, distracted, went off after it. The evidence for the story is found on the island of O'ahu at Koko Head, where a hill inland from Hanauma Bay, aptly named Kohelepelepe (detached vagina) shows on its eastern side the imprint made where Kapo's decoy struck against it.

Kamapua'a could not get his mind off his desire for Pele. He went to woo her, but she scorned him, calling him a pig and a son of a pig, and even more insulting jibes. Their taunts led to a furious battle between them.

She hurled fire and molten lava at him and chased him into the sea, but he turned himself into a little fish, the *humuhumu-nukunuku-'ā-pua'a*, whose tough skin protected him from the boiling heat when the lava poured into the sea.

Again he approached her, and again she attacked. He retaliated with storms of rain and called up great numbers of tusked hogs which overran her lands, rooting destructively. The cloudbursts almost doused her fires. When her brothers saw that Pele was losing, and that the deluge threatened to

extinguish her fires and soak the sacred fire sticks, they intervened and ordered her to yield.

A place near the coast in Puna called Ka-lua-o-Pele, where the land seems torn up as if a great struggle had taken place, is said to be where Kamapuaʻa had his way with her.

As may sometimes happen with opposites, Pele decided to take him as her lover. Togetherness was not their style, however, so they divided the island between them — Pele taking the drier leeward side where the mountain slopes are streaked with lava flows, and Kamapuaʻa taking the windward side, moist with rain and verdant with growing things.

Yet even on the dry side of the island, on recent lava flows, we may see how Pele must always yield to Kamapuaʻa. Seeds will come, rains will germinate them, vigorous roots will penetrate the barren lava, breaking it up over thousands of years until it becomes fertile soil. Pele may build the island with her lava, but it is the incessant attentions of Kamapuaʻa that make it fertile.

Such are the interactions of opposites that have given form to the world. But they are relationships which are seldom tranquil. It is said that they had a child who became an ancestor of chiefs and commoners. It is also said that Kamapuaʻa tired of it all, and sailed off to another place.

Other lovers of Pele, however, did not make such a clean getaway. Too late, they would discover that she would tolerate no competition. If she found them with other women she would overwhelm them with lava. There are many curious lava formations throughout her domain which are the alleged remains of these unfortunates.

FOLK TALES

The mountain slopes of Pele's domain are forested by *'ōhi'a-lehua.* The tree is named *'ohi'a,* and its blossom is named *lehua.* They were once a man and a woman.

The young man 'Ōhi'a and his beautiful companion Lehua were inseparable lovers. Pele became attracted to 'Ōhi'a and came to him as a lovely young woman, but he had no time for her, his attention being devoted entirely to Lehua. Pele's envy grew into rage and she killed them both.

Reproached by her sisters, her anger cooled and she grieved over what she had done. Repentant, she turned 'Ōhi'a's body into a tree, and Lehua's body into the flower of that tree. That is why the rough-barked *'ōhi'a* tree is of masculine appearance, whereas the feathery *lehua* blossom which flowers upon the *'ōhi'a* seems softly feminine. In this way the two lovers have become as inseparable for eternity as they once were in mortal life.

Ohia and Lehua; bas reliefs, designed by Herb Kane, carved by Christian Sorensen. C. Brewer Collection.

Two girls were roasting breadfruit when an old woman approached them asking for food and water. One of the girls gladly shared what she had, but the other refused with the excuse that her food had been consecrated to the goddess Laka.

Soon afterwards a flood of lava came through their district. The stingy girl's home was consumed, but the generous girl's home was spared.

Hōlua was the sport of racing narrow sleds with long hard-wood runners down long slides built up of rockwork and thatched with slippery grasses, probably laid over a shingling of coarse mats. It was a dangerous sport in which only chiefs participated.

Near Kapoho in the Puna district, at the summit of a *hōlua* slide, a proud young chief named Kahāwali was approached by a strange woman who challenged him to a race. He refused without bothering to be polite, and launched his sled down the slide. Hearing screams from the spectators below and a

roaring sound behind him, he glanced back and saw the woman pursuing him all aflame, riding a flow of fiery lava.

Knowing that the woman he had scorned was none other than Pele, Kahāwali used all his skill to gain speed and keep ahead of her. At the base of the slide he leaped from his sled and dashed for the seashore, the lava hot upon his heels. His brother happened to be there in a canoe. He scrambled into it and they paddled out, narrowly escaping the lava as it rushed into the sea. Certain that he could never be safe on Hawai'i, he raised the sail and fled to Maui.

Pele could not tolerate braggarts. The story is told of a man who, while visiting the volcanoes, boasted to everyone about the superior beauty of his home district. He returned to find it covered with lava flows.

In this century, the story is often told of a man who was driving alone at night over the high road that traverses the saddle between the mountains Mauna Kea and Mauna Loa. In an area of desolate lava and thick fog his headlights revealed the figure of an old Hawaiian woman beside the road. Stopping the car he offered her a ride, and she got into the rear seat.

He drove on, his entire attention on the winding road ahead. After the fog had cleared he remembered his passenger. He politely attempted to start a conversation, but received no reply. Looking over his shoulder, he saw that the rear seat was empty.

HOW PELE HELPED KAMEHAMEHA

In 1790, after seven years of warfare, the remaining contenders for the rule of the Island of Hawai'i were Keoua, son of the late King Kalani'ōpu'u, and his cousin Kamehameha, feared by the ruling chiefs of all the islands as a dangerous upstart. While Kamehameha was campaigning on Maui and Moloka'i, Keoua attacked along the windward coast of Hawai'i, laying waste to districts loyal to Kamehameha.

Kamehameha hastened back to Hawai'i with his fleet and army. After several inconclusive battles, Keoua returned to his home district of Ka'ū. His army marched in three groups, many of the soldiers accompanied by wives and children.

As Keoua, with the first division, was passing Kīlauea volcano, the land was shaken by earthquakes. Keoua made prayers to Pele, and the first division passed through safely. Then, according to the historian S. M. Kamakau, there was a violent

explosion: "A pillar of sand and rock rose straight up in the air — and a flame of fire appeared at its top. It looked as if a little hill were being pushed straight up by a larger one until it burst into masses of sand and rock. The second division of Keoua's army was completely destroyed in a rain of hot ashes, rocks, and poisonous gasses."

The rear contingent hastened forward after the cloud had cleared, rejoicing that they had suffered no injury. But their joy turned to dismay when they discovered their dead comrades lying about in their order of march, unmutilated, as if they were asleep. All were covered with gray ash, some sitting upright and clasping their wives and children to them.

Badly shaken by this disaster, no doubt believing that Pele had turned against him, Keoua lost the will to continue the war.

At that time Kamehameha was completing a great temple to his war god Kū-kā'ili-moku. Named Pu'ukoholā, it was sited upon a hill overlooking Kawaihae Bay in the Kohala district. The project was a masterpiece of psychological warfare, for his enemies believed that if Kamehameha could complete it, the full power of his war god would be bestowed upon him. The ruling chiefs of Kaua'i, O'ahu, and Maui sent a combined fleet against Hawai'i, but they were met at sea by Kamehameha's fleet and defeated. When the temple was completed, Kamehameha sent emissaries to Keoua, inviting him to come and meet with him.

The Building of Pu'ukohola Heiau

Keoua accepted. Fey of spirit, heedless of the warnings of his advisors, he sailed with his fleet northward along the western coast of Hawai'i to Kawaihae Bay. Stopping along the way to perform purification rites, he told those who would sail in his canoe to bring no weapons and to prepare themselves to be his companions in death.

Kamehameha was waiting on the beach with a crowd of his men as the fleet sailed into the bay below the temple. Walking out into the water, Kamehameha called to Keoua to come ashore and converse with him. But as Keoua stepped out of his canoe, the impetuous Kona chief Ke'eaumoku, in sudden fury, leaped forward and threw his spear. Before Kamehameha could stop the fighting that followed, Keoua and all but one of those who were on his canoe had been killed. Those in the other canoes of Keoua's fleet were permitted to depart in peace.

Keoua's body was taken to the temple, Pu'ukoholā, as a sacrifice. The news of his death added to the consternation of Kamehameha's enemies. But whether Kamehameha had planned to kill his rival, or had honestly invited him to discuss peace, remains unresolved.

The Arrival of Keoua

A Ceremony at the Heiau

Eleven years later, in 1801, when Kamehameha was peacefully ruling his new kingdom from his capitol at Kailua in the Kona District, an eruption on Mt. Hualalai spread a flow of lava down its flanks that destroyed many villages and fishponds along the Kona coast north of Kailua. The offerings and prayers of the priests were all in vain; the flow continued, widening and doing great destruction. Advised by a priest of the Pele cult that he must make propitiative sacrifices himself, Kamehameha sailed north to where the lava was entering the sea at Mahai'ula.

The most precious gift a ruling chief could make to a god was the life of a man; but this could only be given to the god Ku, patron of men and their work, warfare, and politics. Pele could not receive human sacrifice. The highest gift Kamehameha could offer was some part of his own body. He cut off a lock of his hair, wrapped it in a *ti* leaf, and with a prayer tossed it into the glowing lava.

Shortly therafter, the flow stopped. The people saw this as confirmation of his power, and the incident gave Kamehameha immense prestige. Indeed, Mount Hualalai has not erupted since.

That is not to say, however, that the mountain will not erupt again. Despite the optimism of those who have recently been covering its slopes with subdivisions, geologists count Hualalai among Hawai'i's active volcanoes, and have stated that an eruption is long overdue. And Kamehameha can no longer be called upon to make peace with Pele.

A CHRISTIAN PRINCESS DEFIES PELE

Soon after the death of Kamehameha in 1819 the Hawaiian religion, one in which there was no distinction between church and state, was formally abolished by the monarchy. Forty years of contact with foreigners had shaken the confidence of Hawaiians in their gods.

Hawaiians sailed on foreign ships and returned with tales of continents swarming with huge populations. Ruling chiefs saw that unless they became Europeanized quickly and won foreign recognition as an independent nation, their small islands would be devoured by some foreign power. This meant the abandonment of the state religion.

Those chiefs who refused to accept this decision made a circuit of the island, raising an army and marching toward the capitol at Kailua in Kona. But the government forces marched out to meet them, and in a furious battle at Keauhou they were destroyed. The old religion and the old gods went out in a blaze of musket fire.

American missionaries arrived a few months later. Expecting resistance, they were surprised to find that the way had been opened for them.

Some elements of the old religion went underground or were preserved in the folkways of the people, where fragments persist today, modified by Christian thought. On the Island of Hawai'i, the disenfranchised priests and priestesses of Pele clung to their roles in open defiance of the new laws. Some action against them seemed necessary.

The high chiefess Kapi'olani, an ardent convert to Christianity who had helped establish a mission near her home at Kealakekua Bay, decided to act in defiance of Pele as a demonstration to her people of the power of her new faith. She journeyed to the Kīlauea volcano accompanied by many friends and retainers. When others attempted to dissuade her, she replied that if she were destroyed they could continue to believe in Pele, but if she were not harmed they must all turn to the one true God.

At the volcano a priestess of Pele attempted to discourage her with dire warnings. Kapi'olani responded by reading passages from the Bible, then descended into the caldera, leading her procession to the brink of the fire-pit Halema'uma'u. Here she ate 'ōhelo berries without first requesting Pele's permission. Proclaiming her faith in the Christian God, she then threw stones into the lake of molten lava below.

Unharmed, she returned to her home, hopeful that her action would help win converts among her people.

Overleaf: Kapiolani Defying Pele

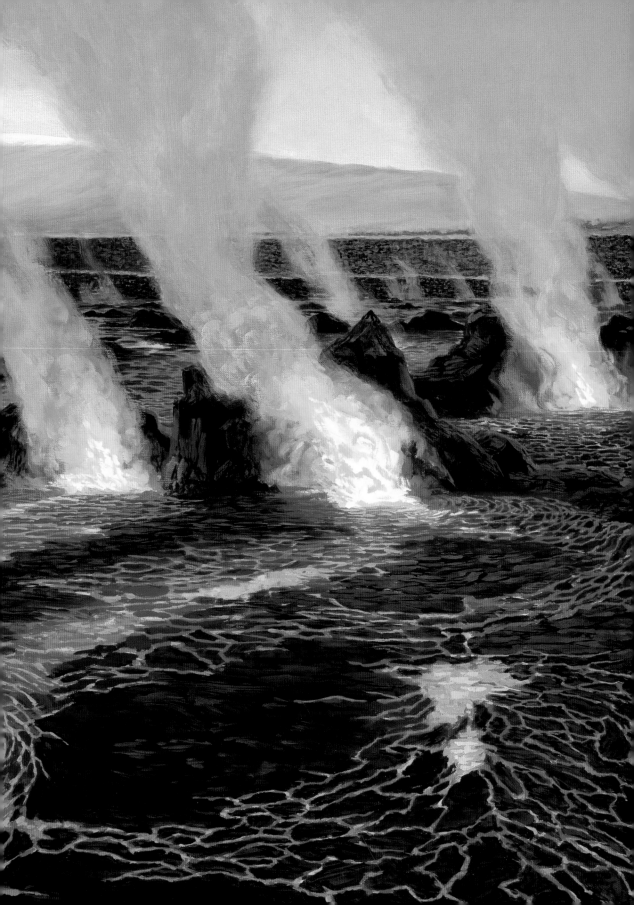

A PRINCESS PROPITIATES PELE

Hawaiians who accepted the new religion still held Pele in reverent awe.

In 1881, when a lava flow from Mauna Loa threatened the city of Hilo, Princess Ruth Ke'elikōlani sailed from Honolulu to Hilo, where she was welcomed by a throng of thousands. She then ascended the mountain to the edge of the advancing lava. A large woman with a stern countenance made more forbidding by a broken nose, she was an impressive figure of regal authority. Throwing many gifts into the lava, she chanted to Pele in a voice that rang above the sound of the lava flow.

The flow soon stopped.

THE SURF RIDER OF PUNALU'U

The cataclysm of 1868 was the most destructive to the Ka'ū District of any volcanic event in historic times. On March 27, a column of smoke rose above Mauna Loa and a stream of lava rushed down its western slope. Tremendous earthquakes shook the land for three days, toppling houses and churches, and whole cliffsides fell into the sea. On April 2, there came a quake which made it impossible for persons and animals to stand upright. Houses were destroyed and a number of people were killed. This was followed by landslides and mudslides that buried houses and plantations, and a series of *tsunami* (tidal waves) swept ten coastal villages out to sea, killing 49 persons — "washed away by the great sea caused by the Woman of the Pit."[1]

At the coastal village of Punalu'u all who survived the first wave ran away from the sea to higher ground. A man named Holoua remembered that he had left his money in his house. Seeing that it had not yet been swept away he rushed back to get it, heedless of his wife's pleading.

While he was in the house the next wave engulfed it and the receding flood took it out to sea. After a time the people saw him climb out of the house and hoist himself up on the roof. Tearing off a wide board from the shattered house, he caught another wave and rode it to shore with his wallet in his teeth.

[1]C.J. Waialoha, *Ka Nupepea Ku'oko'a*, April 11, 1868.

For the rest of his life he claimed that he was the only Hawaiian he knew who could hang on to his money.

THE MAN WHOSE FAITH WAS STRONG

In my father's youth, the old folks used to tell the tale of an incident that was believed to have occurred several generations earlier. An American sea captain — my father did not hear his name — had retired from the sea and started a ranch on the slopes of Mauna Loa.

While riding over his land he found in a cave a stone of curious shape resting on a mat. He took it home and set it up in his garden.

His Hawaiian cowboys begged him to take it back, averring that this was an object sacred to the worship of Pele. If he returned it quickly, or let them return it and make some observances of respect over it, Pele might be appeased.

Being a strong Christian, he refused. Compliance with their request would, he feared, be interpreted by the Hawaiians as his recognition of Pele's existence. He rebuked them as part-time

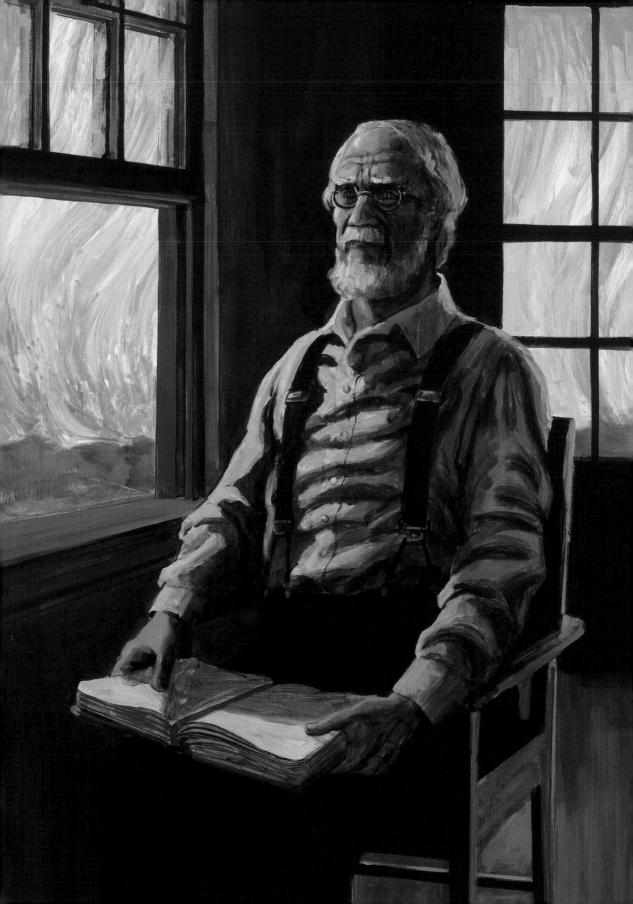

Christians, part-time pagans who only went to church because they enjoyed the singing and socializing. Pele did not exist; therefore the stone could have no importance.

Shortly thereafter Mauna Loa erupted and a stream of lava covered a corner of his ranch, then moved off in another direction. Now the Hawaiians came to him in great consternation, begging that he give them the stone. Again he refused and sent them away.

Then, as the eruption continued, the flow resumed its earlier course, covering much of his land and approaching his house. That evening the Hawaiians came again. When the rancher again refused to give them the stone they urged him to come away with them; but he replied that his safety rested in Jesus, that he would remain in his house and pray to the True God and be saved. Having no further argument the Hawaiians mounted their horses and rode off into the darkness.

Pray he did, Bible in hand throughout the night, as the lava approached his house. Trees flared and exploded as their sap turned to steam, and clouds of smoke billowed upward, red in the glow of molten rock. His house was filled with smoke and the heat from the flow made it an oven. He continued to pray..

The next day the flow stopped. When the Hawaiians approached they found that it had separated into two fingers which had passed his house, leaving it standing on a small peninsula, a little rise in the land by which they could reach him. They found him sitting in his house with his Bible clenched in his hands and a fierce expression upon his face.

"Now you have seen the power of God," he said. "I am saved. What do you think of your Pele now?"

"We too have prayed to the God of Jesus," his foreman replied, "and we rejoice that you are alive. But we must confess that the stone is no longer in your garden.

"As we left you last night, we took it away and returned it to its proper place and made a chant of respect to the Woman of the Pit. Perhaps she does not exist, as you say. But when our friend was in such danger, we wanted to do everything we could to help him."

It was said that the man was never the same after that. A madness came over him. He sold out for what little he could get for his ravaged land and moved to Honolulu.

TALES FROM MARY KAWENA PUKUI

One of Hawai'i's most gifted scholars, Mary Kawena Pukui (1895 - 1986), was born and raised in the Ka'ū. The following are excerpts from her contributions to the Bernice P. Bishop Museum Bulletin 233 (1972), *Native Planters in Old Hawai'i*[2]:

"Uncle Napua (the youngest brother of Auntie Keli'ihue) was a person who saw and heard more than most people in the district of Ka'ū, so when he made unusual statements, his fellow Hawaiians accepted them.

"One day, after taking some Mormon elders to upper Kam'oa, he sat down to wait with the horses while the elders went on to visit some of the members who lived beyond. Soon Napua heard the horses snort and paw the ground, and coming toward them was a woman he did not recognize. She asked him for a cigarette, which she smoked so fast that it vanished before his own was even half-smoked. As soon as she turned to go, she said to him, "I am going to Kona, and by next week, you will hear news from Papa." He watched her go, and to his amazement saw that instead of walking on the trail, she seemed to be floating about a foot above it. He knew then that she was no ordinary woman. Exactly a week later to that very day, a lava flow went down from Moku'aweoweo to Papa in Kona.

"The woman Napua saw was Pele."

"We Hawaiians have no explanation for the *popo-ahi*, or "fireball," yet we have seen it. It has no connection whatever with the *akua-lele*, or poison gods, that traveled at night, nor does it have a tail that sends out sparks as it travels.

"I had frequently heard of it in Ka'ū, but it was while I was in Glenwood, Ola'a, that I saw it, like a round pale moon, moving slowly from the direction of Kīlauea to Mauna Loa. The older folks with me said very quietly, 'She [Pele] is moving to her home at Moku'āweoweo. Let us see what is going to happen.' When, a week later, news came that Moku'āweoweo was active, they nodded knowlingly — yes, they had seen the old lady travel and knew that that was exactly what was going to happen."

Many other stories are told of Pele's appearances, often presaging earthquakes and volcanic eruptions. In May, 1924, residents of the village of Waiohinu in the southern Ka'ū District of Hawai'i reported seeing a tall Hawaiian woman, a stranger dressed in a flowing white garment, walking about the countryside. Beautiful and stately, she passed by all who saw her, speaking to no one.

Soon afterward there were great earthquakes and Kīlauea exploded, throwing out huge rocks and sending up a cloud of dust and gasses that rose to twenty thousand feet. Chasms opened in the earth, and along the southeastern coast the land subsided, in some places as much as fourteen feet.

PELE'S FIRST FOREIGN VISITOR

E Pele, eia ka 'ōhelo 'au;
e taumaha aku wau 'ia 'oe,
e 'ai ho'i au tetahi.

Oh, Pele, here are your *'ōhelo* berries;
I offer some to you,
some I also eat.

Wm. Ellis

This was a Hawaiian tribute to Pele heard and recorded by the first foreign visitor to the volcanoes, the American missionary William Ellis, in 1823. The berries had looked tempting to Ellis and his companions, and, " ...experiencing both hunger and thirst, we eagerly plucked and ate all that came in our way.

"As soon as the natives perceived us eating them, they called out aloud, and begged us to desist, saying that we were now within the precincts of Pele's dominions, to whom they belonged, and by whom they were *rahui'ia* (prohibited), until some had been offered her and permission to eat them asked. We told them we were sorry they should feel uneasy on this account — that we acknowledged Jehovah as the only divine proprietor of the fruits of the earth, and felt thankful to Him for them, especially in our present circumstances.

Quotations are from the *Journal of William Ellis,* Reprint of the London 1827 Edition and the Hawaii 1917 Edition; Advertiser Publishing Co. Ltd. Honolulu 1963

"The South-West End of the Volcano of Kirauea, in 1823" Engraving from a sketch by Ellis

"Some of them then said, 'We are afraid. We shall be overtaken by some calamity before we leave this place.'

"We advised them to dismiss their fears and eat with us, as we knew they were thirsty and faint. They shook their heads, and perceiving us determined to disregard their entreaties, walked along in silence.

"We travelled on, regretting that the natives should indulge notions so superstitious, but clearing every *ʻōhelo* bush that grew near our path, till about two p.m. when the Crater of Kirauea* suddenly burst upon our view."

Ellis's guides then plucked several branches. Walking to the edge of the crater, they "...turned their faces toward the place where the greatest quantity of smoke and vapour issued, and, breaking the branch they held in their hand in two, they threw one part down the precipice..." saying at the same time the chant which Ellis recorded.

"Several of them told us, as they turned around from the crater, that after such acknowledgments they might eat the fruit with security."

*In Ellis's time the classical "r" as in "Kirauea" was beginning to change to the modern "l", as in "Kilauea".

Ellis and his companions were led by their Hawaiian guides to the caldera of Kīlauea, "...a vast plain before us, fifteen or sixteen miles in circumference, and sunk from 200 to 400 feet below its original level — and in the centre of it was the great crater. Our guides led us round towards the north end of the ridge, in order to find a place by which we might descend to the plain below."

They descended into the caldera. "...We came at length to the edge of the great crater, where a spectacle, sublime and even appalling, presented itself before us.

"We stopped, and trembled.

"Astonishment and awe for some moments rendered us mute, and, like statues, we stood fixed to the spot, with our eyes riveted on the abyss below.

"Immediately before us yawned an immense gulf, in the form of a crescent, about two miles in length — nearly a mile in width, and apparently 800 feet deep.

"The bottom was covered with lava...one vast flood of burning matter, in a state of terrific ebullition, rolling to and fro its fiery surge of flaming billows.

"Fifty-one conical islands, of varied form and size, rose from the surface of the burning lake.

"Twenty-two constantly emitted columns of gray smoke, or pyramids of brilliant flame; and several of these at the same time vomited from their ignited mouths streams of lava, which rolled in blazing torrents down their black indented sides into the boiling mass below."

Conforming the experience to his religious convictions, Ellis wrote: "After the first feelings of astonishment had subsided, we remained a considerable time contemplating a scene, which it is impossible to describe, and which filled us with wonder and admiration at the almost overwhelming manifestation it affords of the power of that dread Being who created the world, and who has declared that by fire he will one day destroy it."

As the first foreigner to witness and write about the volcano, Ellis's description was similar to those written by the host of writers who would come later, including the oft-quoted Mark Twain. Like Ellis, some would admit that the scene "was impossible to describe," then set down pages of purple prose in an attempt to do so.

Ellis was the first to make a written record; but others, many centuries earlier, had made their own discovery of the volcanoes.

Like Ellis, they saw in the power and majesty of the volcanoes a personality capable of creation as well as destruction. Unlike Ellis, they saw not the "dread Being" of his formidable brand of Christianity, a Being who would someday destroy the world, but the spirit of their ancestral relative Pele.

THE CURSE OF PELE

The beauty of lava glistening in the sunlight may produce in visitors an irresistible temptation to pop a few pretty rocks into their bags and take them home as souvenirs.

There is a belief that bad luck will follow any visitors who take away pieces of Pele's lava. No one knows how it began. Some say tour conductors started it to discourage their customers from littering their vehicles with rocks and sand; others aver — without supporting evidence — that the tradition is ancient.

The tradition may have grown from the Hawaiian policy of refraining from any acts that might be disrespectful to Pele. Missionaries, following their own policy, treated such customs with contempt at every opportunity. This led to confrontations.

The missionary Hiram Bingham described a "prophetess" of Pele, a *haka* (medium) "even calling herself Pele," who approached in a fury, "...marching with a haughty step, with long, black, dishevelled hair and countenance wild, with spear and *kāhili* (feathered standard) in her hands."[3] She accused the missionaries of offending Pele by eating 'ōhelo berries without first making offerings to Pele, by rolling stones into the crater, and by taking away bits of Pele's hair (brown glass filaments made when volcanic glass blows through highly fluid lava). She demanded that the missionaries be sent home.

---

3 Bingham, Hiram; *A Residence of Twenty-One Years in the Sandwich Islands;* Hartford: Huntington, 1847

Misfortune will certainly fall upon anyone within National Park boundaries whose collecting efforts happen to be witnessed by a Park Ranger, for it is illegal to remove anything from the Volcanoes National Park without permission. But the origin of the tradition that Pele's curse will follow such collectors remains a mystery.

The Hawai'i Volcanoes National Park frequently receives packages containing rocks or other volcanic products, usually accompanied by plaintive letters describing the bad luck that has plagued the senders since they picked up their bits of lava as souvenirs. A few of these tales of woe are on display at the Park Visitor Center. The following are typical:

"On a trip to Hawai i I deliberately took the enclosed rock of lava from the volcano, knowing the legend of the god Pele (I don't quite remember it now) but I was warned that it would bring me bad luck. Not being a person believing in good or bad luck I thought I might defy the superstition and bring it with me as a good luck piece.

"Five years later, ten car accidents later, two unsuccessful business ventures later, and twice-broken heart later, I admit that the place for the enclosed rock of lava is there where it belongs.

"Thank you in advance for returning the rock to the mountain."

"I send the enclosed lava rocks to Madame Pele. They belong to her. I picked them up in 1937 while serving with the U.S. Army. Now maybe my luck will change."

"I read all the letters in your case from visitors who had taken lava rocks home with them with some amusement. Unfortunately I'm not finding it amusing anymore. After we returned with a small vial of black sand my husband has been hospitalized twice and has lost his job. Cars, TVs, and various household appliances have broken down and we seem to be having a streak of bad luck as we never had before. I'm now among the ranks of believers."

"Well, here's another testimonial for your file. In spite of the warnings we read while on the Big Island, we picked up some pieces of lava rock at several road cuts on the south and southwestern part of the island. These were to be souvenirs for ourselves and our friends. We were on Hawai'i in December, 1982.

"Since we returned to Denver we've had a monstrous snowstorm which ruined our family reunion here at Christmas. My sister and I had the first big fight of our lives and we are still not speaking to each other. Today another big snowstorn has ruined the grand opening of my wife's new business.

"Well, enough is enough. We are returning to Pele all of the rocks and all of the pieces of coral we took too, just in case. Please entreat her to release us from her terrible spell."

THE WARNING

From 1954 to 1965, Radio KIPA in Hilo featured a weekday interview and music show hosted by Betty Curtiss (now Kukuna De Aguiar).

In 1960, Betty took two friends on a tour of Volcanoes National Park. In the evening they stopped at the Volcano House Hotel for dinner. They waited in the main lounge for the dining room to open, amidst a noisy crowd of tourists.

While standing in front of the fireplace in conversation with her friends, Betty felt a sharp twinge in the back of her neck, as if someone had jabbed her with a fingernail or needle. Turning, she saw an elderly Hawaiian lady wearing a white *holoku* (a full-length nineteenth century dress with a train that is traditional formal wear in Hawai'i) approaching through the crowd. Those who were in her way moved to let her pass, but otherwise seemed to take no notice of her.

"Are you Betty Curtiss?" asked the elderly lady.

"Yes, I am."

"Are you the announcer who made the broadcast from Kapoho?"

Betty had made a radio broadcast from the site of the eruption that had destroyed the village of Kapoho in January of that year.

"Yes, Tūtū. How can I help you?"

The elderly lady stared at Betty for a long moment, then said: "Within thirty days, the island will be visited by either Hina or Pele —" her voice dropped, and she continued: " — and the results will be catastrophic."

With that she turned an walked away. As before, the crowd parted to let her pass without seeming to take notice of her.

"Well, how about that?" Betty said, turning back to her companions.

"How about what?" one asked.

"The elderly Hawaiian lady I was talking to."

Betty's friends had seen her turn away from them, but had not seen the Hawaiian woman, and in the noisy room they had not overheard any of the conversation.

It is a matter of record that for the following five days, after the noon news, Betty repeated the dire prediction to her radio audience.

Twenty-eight days after her encounter, a *tsunami* was generated by a fault movement off the coast of Chile. Travelling with such speed that it reached Hawai'i in 15 hours, the wave struck along the southern and eastern coasts. At Hilo, it drove water to heights as great as 35 feet, wiped out a large area of the town, and killed 61 persons.

NOW YOU SEE HER, NOW YOU DON'T

On the night of July 5, 1975, I was aboard Hokule'a, a replica of a Polynesian voyaging canoe anchored in Honaunau Bay, South Kona. The double-hulled sailing canoe had been built on O'ahu, and I had skippered it on a training and shakedown cruise to Maui, then on to Hawai'i. It was a peaceful night. The canoe gently swung at its anchor in the tranquil little cove, and the black water reflected bright stars. I happened to glance up at the stars, and saw the sky over Mauna Loa turn red.

My friend Dr. Jack Lockwood, a geologist with the U.S. Geological Survey's Hawai'i Volcano Observatory, obtained a better view. He happened to be flying a light plane over Mauna Loa, and was first to see the fountaining of lava at its summit crater, Moku'āweoweo. It was the first eruption of this gigantic crater in twenty six years, and it lasted eighteen hours.

There is a long and arduous hiking trail that climbs to Mauna Loa's 13,680 foot summit. Because earthquakes during and after the eruption made the summit area very dangerous, the trail was closed.

On a daylight helicopter flight to the summit, Jack and Reginald Okamura, also of the Observatory, were surprised to see three persons at the Pu'u 'Ula'ula rest cabin below the crater. The area was dangerous and had been declared off-limits to hikers. Two were standing in front of the cabin, and a third, a woman, was on the porch. He radioed Park Headquarters and another helicopter was sent to bring them out. He assumed that it would take two flights to bring out the three persons.

But the helicopter only made one flight, bringing out two hikers who, on being questioned, said that they had been alone at the cabin and had seen no woman there.

Jack and Reggie did not make a close observation of the woman, but it did seem unusual to them that she was barefooted.

KURE MIDWAY

100 MILLION YEARS AGO
At a "hot spot" in Earth's crust magma from
earth's core blasts upward through the Pacific
Plate, building volcanoes which become
seamounts or islands.

VOLCANO COUNTRY

The Island of Hawai'i is larger than all the other islands in
the Hawaiian archipelago put together. The others have been
eroding away over millions of years, and some have
disappeared altogether, reduced to shoals or pinnacles inhabited
by birds and seals. But Hawai'i is still growing.

Geologists believe that tiny Kure and Midway, thousands of
miles to the northwest, were once, perhaps forty million years
ago, at the same spot on the globe now occupied by Hawai'i.
Here they were built by magma from below the Earth's crust
rising through a fracture, a "hot spot" in Earth's crust, and
penetrating up through the Pacific Plate which lies at the
bottom of our planet's largest ocean.

The Pacific Plate is not stationary; it has been sliding slowly
northwestward, and as each island was formed it was carried
away from the "hot spot," and another formed in its place.

Hawai'i's northern volcanoes, the Kohala Mountains and
Mauna Kea (13,800 feet above sea level), are now considered to
be dormant. Active volcanoes are Mt. Hualalai in Kona,
Mauna Loa, and Kīlauea at 4,000 feet on the southern slope of

GROWTH AND EROSION OF AN ISLAND

SUBMARINE SEAMOUNT   SHIELD-BUILDING STAGE   CALDERA STAGE

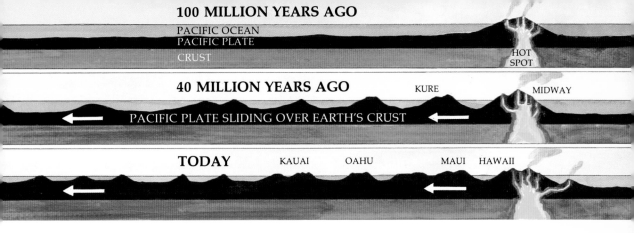

100 MILLION YEARS AGO

PACIFIC OCEAN
PACIFIC PLATE
CRUST

HOT SPOT

40 MILLION YEARS AGO KURE MIDWAY

PACIFIC PLATE SLIDING OVER EARTH'S CRUST

TODAY KAUAI OAHU MAUI HAWAII

40 MILLION YEARS AGO

As the Pacific Plate slides over the underlying crust, an assembly line of volcanoes is built over the hot spot, and carried to the northwest. 40 million years ago the island now known as Kure and Midway were much larger islands building where Hawai'i is now.

TODAY

The sliding Pacific Plate has carried Midway more than 2,200 miles from its original location. Erosion has reduced the older islands to small islands, coral atolls, pinnacles, or shoals. Hawai'i is now building where Midway once emerged. South of Hawai'i the seamount Loihi is building and may become another island in 10,000 years.

Mauna Loa. Of these, Kīlauea is most active, and the crater Halema'uma'u within the gigantic Kīlauea caldera is traditionally Pele's home.

Measured from its base at the ocean floor, Mauna Kea ("white mountain") is the highest mountain in the world. Mauna Loa ("long mountain"), only a few hundred feet lower, by its great mass is thought to be the largest volcano in the world.

South of Hawai'i, its summit beneath the sea, another volcano is growing. Named Loihi, it is expected to surface in about 10,000 years.

The Volcanoes National Park extends from the southern shore of Hawai'i to the summit of Mauna Loa, and is centered at Kīlauea. Visitors driving to Kīlauea approach from the eastern town of Hilo or the western district of Kona, ascending from a tropical environment at sea level through upland plantations and ranches to mountain forests of *'ōhi'a* and ferns. Those who come from Kona pass over many lava flows, some very recent.

EROSION

CORAL GROWTH

EROSION & REEF-BUILDING
EXPANDING CORAL REEF

LAGOON

CORAL ATOLL STAGE
CORAL REEF & ISLES

LAGOON

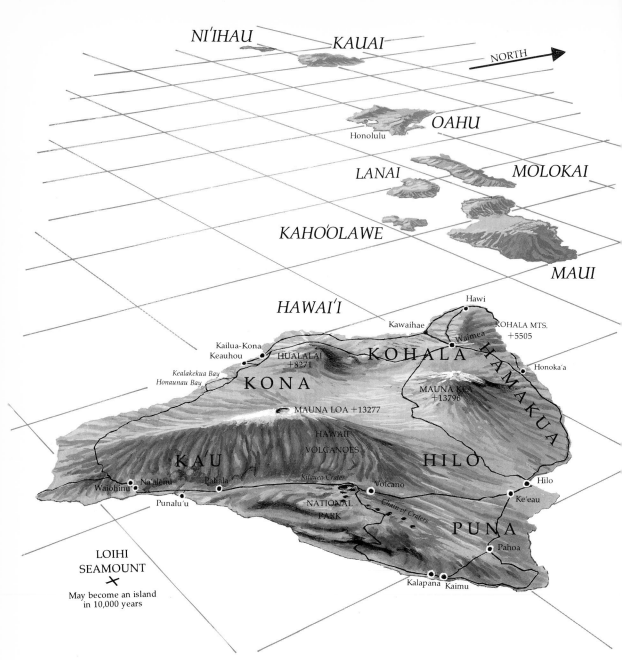

NI'IHAU

KAUAI

NORTH

OAHU

Honolulu

LANAI

MOLOKAI

KAHO'OLAWE

MAUI

HAWAI'I

Hawi

Kawaihae

KOHALA MTS.
+5505

Kailua-Kona
Keauhou

HUALALAI
+8271

KOHALA

Waimea

HAMAKUA

Honoka'a

Kealakekua Bay
Honaunau Bay

KONA

MAUNA KEA
+13796

MAUNA LOA +13277

HAWAI'I
VOLCANOES

KA'U

Kīlauea Crater

HILO

Hilo

Waiohinu

Na'alehu

Pahala

Volcano

Ke'eau

Punalu'u

NATIONAL
PARK

Chain of Craters

PUNA

Pahoa

LOIHI
SEAMOUNT
✕
May become an island
in 10,000 years

Kalapana

Kaimu

Within the National Park the landscape shifts abruptly from lunar deserts to mountain meadows to misty forests, and ultimately to the great smoking caldera of Kīlauea. Here is a land of craters, banks of golden sulfur, plumes of steam rising from cracks in the earth, lava caves, tree-like ferns, glistening new lava flows, great cones built by fountains of lava, fields of ash and pumice where grow the *'ōhelo* berries sacred to Pele, forests of rough-barked *'ōhi'a* trees aflame with feathery red *lehua* blossoms.

From the Park Headquarters a road descends past a chain of craters and new lava flows to the sea, and to the ancient temple of Waha'ula. Or you may drive up the slope of Mauna Loa above Kīlauea through forests of stately *koa* to the lower end of a hiking trail that leads high above the treeline, through alpine regions, to desolate Moku'aweoweo Crater at the mountain's summit, often covered with snow.

All of these wonders will get less of your attention if an eruption is taking place, especially one that can be safely approached and viewed.

PAINTING IN PUBLIC

Within Pele's domain, the sparsely inhabited districts of Puna and Ka'ū probably produce more tales of "spooky stuffs" than any other areas of the Hawaiian Islands.

In 1973 I was living in Honolulu and working as a design consultant to C. Brewer, a major landholder in Ka'ū. I had participated with my client's architects and with designer-photographer Boone Morrison in the design of a restaurant and small history museum that was now being built at Punalu'u, on the edge of a freshwater pond that lay behind a beach of black sand. This was the site of the village that had been destroyed by the *tsunami* of 1868.

A planned feature of the "history center" was a mural depicting how Punalu'u might have appeared two centuries ago, when it was a village of thatched houses. The setting of the village, the pond, and the beach were to be shown with figures: women working under a thatched shelter; fishermen coming ashore, some working on a canoe; men preparing to bake a pig in an earth oven; chiefs and a priest on the beach awaiting the

landing of the double-hulled sailing canoe of a visiting chief —
all the activity that might have filled the scene at Punaluʻu on a
sunny day long ago. On the far side of the cove, beyond the
surf, the great rock platform of the *heiau* (temple), known as Kā-
neʻeleʻele, would be depicted as it may have appeared then, with
thatched structures, fences of palings, and carved temple
images. The mural would be painted on a curved wall ten feet
high, twenty feet long, and cushioned to take the shock of
earthquakes. Construction superintendent Kumio Matsumoto
saw that the wall was built and plastered correctly, and when all
was ready I went to Kaʻū.

Coming from the bustle of modern Honolulu to the rural
island of my childhood, some culture shock was experienced. I
rented a little house in the countryside near the village of Waiohinu, took my meals at Roy Toguchi's restaurant in the village
of Naʻalehu (the sign proclaims that it is the southernmost com-
munity in the U.S.), and occasionally saw wild pigs crossing the
road on my morning drive to the construction site.

While Boone and his crew were constructing the historical displays, and others were working on the restaurant and on the landscaping that was being installed around the cluster of buildings, I began the mural.

Soon I had visitors. The other workers came by to see what was happening. Then, as word spread, residents of Ka'ū began to drop in to see what "da paintah" was doing. Some had questions, but most were content to stand behind me silently while I worked. My first impulse was to chase them all away, but they really were little bother to me. My work held my attention. Much of the time I was not aware of my audience until I would happen to turn away from the painting and see them, standing quietly and smiling.

I made friends, and I began to learn about Ka'ū. The subject matter of the painting brought out stories about Ka'ū as it once was, especially from the older folk. The elderly Mary Kawena Pukui, a distinguished Hawaiian scholar, dropped by on a visit to the place of her childhood, and told me the legend of Kauila, the gentle turtle-mermaid who once inhabited the freshwater pond that lay between the construction site and the beach. This became the subject of a painting which would hang in the restaurant, overlooking the pond.

Some of the workers would come by with beer after work and "talk story." When I worked into the night, families would come by after their dinner. My visitors would sit or stand behind me in the shadows, away from my work light, and sometimes they would tell stories. Some were of the kind that I had heard as a child in Waipi'o Valley, on nights when the old folks sat out on the veranda and told tales that could make a child too frightened to get out of bed to pee at night.

Being in Ka'ū, away from the smug modernity of Honolulu, was like being in a time warp.

There came a time when some expensive electronic displays were being installed, so at night all doors were locked except the door that opened to the section in which I was working, and the security guard would lock this door also when I was not there. One night, returning to work after dinner, I had him unlock the door for me. He turned on the lights and together we walked through the building to see the progress that had been made by those who were installing the displays. Then he went out. I turned out all the lights except my work lights, and went to work.

I had worked for perhaps an hour, when I turned from my work and saw an elderly Hawaiian woman standing in the shadows, looking at the painting. I said, "Good evening."

She did not reply, but smiled, looking not at me but at the painting. I returned to my work. A few minutes later I looked back, but she wasn't there.

I worked for a few more minutes, then decided to quit. Outside the guard was sitting on a bench.

"That old *tūtū*-lady who was just here. She looked pure Hawaiian. Does she live around here?" I asked.

"What lady?" He replied. "I've been sitting here for half an hour and nobody has come in or out that door. Are you okay?"

Thinking it over, I found an explanation for what had happened — or seemed to happen. When one is deeply immersed in painting, time whips by at appalling speed. It is entirely possible that the old woman had visited me much earlier in the evening, coming and going while the guard was making his rounds. After her visit, that which seemed to be only a few minutes could have been a much longer span of time. I preferred to believe that this was what really happened.

Perhaps a week later, after six weeks of work, the painting was nearing completion. I started work early one day, and worked through the day with no meals and only a few short breaks. A class of schoolchildren came to see the mural, but there were not many other visitors.

I kept at it because the painting was going well. It was one of those rare times when the brush seems to move itself, and I wanted to keep it moving. That night an electronics technician from Maui, Steve Rose, was working on a display on the other side of the building, whistling and singing as he worked.

It was a noisy night, the surf booming upon the beach and the wind rattling palm fronds and branches. At some time after eleven I heard voices. Perhaps someone was visiting Steve. I walked around to his area but his lights were out and he was gone.

I returned to work. A few minutes later I heard the voices again. They were speaking in the Hawaiian language. Now they seemed to be coming from the painting. I turned toward the group of chiefs that I had painted standing upon the beach and saw that they were talking to each other. There was a movement on my left (the painting was on a curved wall) and I turned just as one of the women seated under a thatched shelter turned her head away from me, back to the profile position in which I had painted her.

I washed out my brush, placed it on my palette, and departed.

The next morning I spread paint on my palette, picked up a brush, looked over the painting, and found that there was really nothing more to do to complete it. I could find no part of it where more brush strokes would improve it.

A metaphysical explanation for this event was not acceptable to me. It is said that intense concentration sustained over many hours can produce hallucination, and I settled upon this as the cause of my extraordinary experience. That the painting had been completed on that same night was probably nothing more than coincidence.

In the fall of 1975 I was in Kona, working on a painting in the King Kamehameha Hotel, then under construction, and staying at the Keauhou Beach Hotel. One night there were several severe earthquakes, followed by a wave that did some damage to waterfront homes. After daybreak I called Jimmy Martinson, a C. Brewer foreman in Ka'ū, to find out what had happened at Punalu'u.

"All bust up," he said. "The buildings are still there, but a twenty foot wave came over the beach and through the pond and went right through the place. The restaurant building, the kitchen building, the history center, all smashed inside and full of mud."

"What about the painting?" I asked.

"You better come see this. Funny thing. The water came right through the building, busted up everything, all the displays, pushed it all out the other side. There is a mud line three feet up the wall. But the painting is dry."

"But the painting extends down to the floor. There is no mud on the painting?"

"Not a bit. You better get over here. Everybody just standing around looking at this thing."

I was there within two hours, and Jimmy and a small crowd of workmen and local residents were standing outside the building. Inside, the mud line showed that three or four feet of water had washed through the building. But there was no mud on the painting. It was dry.

I searched for an explanation, but found none.

"Let's face it," someone said. "You live in Ka'ū and you see things happen. You don't try to explain it or you go crazy."

"It's Tūtū, guaranteed," said another. "She make the quake, the quake make the wave."

"You mean Tūtū Pele?" I asked.

"Who else? She always get the last word."